Contents

Burrow babies

Some baby animals

grow up in burrows.

Burrows are

under the ground.

A puffin chick lives in the back of a burrow. **Cheep!** Its parents feed it fish.

Zzz.

A badger cub sleeps.

It wakes up.

It drinks milk from mum.

Baby rabbits need a home.

A rabbit digs a burrow.

She lines it with fur.

Up and down

Prairie dog burrows are big.

Pups grow in one room.

They come up to play.

Baby meerkats look out.

Bark!

Mum warns her pups.

They go back down.

A baby armadillo
looks for food.
Mum helps.
They find some beetles.
They go back in their burrow.

A trapdoor spider looks out.

A bird!

She closes the door.

Her babies stay safe.

Eggs lie in a burrow.

Crack!

Baby desert tortoises crawl out. Hello!

Glossary

armadillo a desert animal with bony plates covering its body

burrow a hole in the ground made or used by an animal

parent a mother or a father

tortoise a reptile with a hard shell

warn to tell about a danger that might happen

Read more

Animals That Dig (Adapted to Survive), Angela Royston (Raintree, 2014)

Inside Rabbit Burrows (Inside Animal Homes), Liz Chung (PowerKids Press, 2016)

Look Inside a Burrow (Look Inside), Richard Spilsbury (Raintree, 2013)

Websites

www.bbc.co.uk/nature/23632577
See photos of animal burrows and learn how to identify which animal made them.

www.bbc.co.uk/nature/life/European_Badger
Learn more about how badgers live, and view videos of badgers.

Comprehension questions

1. How do burrows help keep baby animals safe?

2. Look at the photo on page 17. How do you think the bony plates on the armadillos help to protect them?

Index